This Being Done

poems by

Stephanie L. Harper

Finishing Line Press
Georgetown, Kentucky

This Being Done

Copyright © 2018 by Stephanie L. Harper
ISBN 978-1-63534-551-3 First Edition
All rights reserved under International and Pan-American Copyright Conventions. No part of this book may be reproduced in any manner whatsoever without written permission from the publisher, except in the case of brief quotations embodied in critical articles and reviews.

ACKNOWLEDGMENTS

"Instead," *formidable Woman* (February 2018).
"Rhapsody in Bone," *BONED* (Spring 2018).
"How to Be a Malacologist," *Panoply* (January 2018).
"In Response to My 13 Year-Old Daughter's Letter" and "Live Feed from the SW Florida Eagle Cam," *The Ibis Head Review* (December 2017).
"Imprisoned," *Claudius Speaks* (Fall 2017).
"Tempted," *Figroot* (September 2017).
"Prologue to My Birth," *International Poetry Month 2017*, Bonnie McClellan-Broussard, editor (January 2017).
"An Elegy for Birds & Bees," and "How to Take an Amazing Photo of a Solar Eclipse," *Slippery Elm Literary Journal* (2015 and 2016).
"Anatomy of a Fustercluck," *Rattle Ekphrastic Challenge* (January 2016).
"Brave," *TulipTree* Publications, LLC's 2016 anthology, *Stories That Need to Be Told*.
"Epitaph" (as "The Artifice of Death") and "Alabaster" (as "I am Alabaster"), *Sixfold* (Winter 2014).

Publisher: Leah Maines
Editor: Christen Kincaid
Cover Art: Matthew Harper
Author Photo: Matthew Harper
Cover Design: Elizabeth Maines McCleavy

Printed in the USA on acid-free paper.
Order online: www.finishinglinepress.com
   also available on amazon.com

Author inquiries and mail orders:
Finishing Line Press
P. O. Box 1626
Georgetown, Kentucky 40324
U. S. A.

Table of Contents

How to Be a Malacologist 1

Fight or Flight 2

Anatomy of a Fustercluck 3

Imprisoned 5

Lupercalia 6

Matthew in the Fountain 7

In Response to My 13 Year-Old Daughter's Letter 8

How to Take an Amazing Photo of a Solar Eclipse 9

An Elegy for Birds & Bees 12

Instead 15

Brave 17

Prologue to My Birth 21

Rhapsody in Bone 23

Epitaph 25

Alabaster 27

Tempted 28

Live Feed from the SW Florida Eagle Cam 30

How to Be a Malacologist

Remember when
your child's heart led your head
like a garden snail's head leads its footed belly.

Think back to when you were seven
& your adopted pet / school project, Kiddo,
gnawed away at a slice of banana on a glass slide
as you watched, thunderstruck, from beneath him
(find out on Wikipedia that he was using his *radula*
a structure akin to a tongue used by mollusks to feed).

Recall how proud you were of Kiddo when he not only lost
the school snail race, but redefined it, by turning around
at the half-way point, staying in his own lane, & crossing
the start-line before any of the other snails reached the finish.

Wonder why your teacher didn't mention anything about Kiddo
& his compatriots being hermaphrodites, or how (if they chose)
they could all be both father & mother to their tiny-shelled progeny,
& realize how simple it would have been for her to call a snail's powerful,
innate mechanism of retracting its tentacles into its head for protection
by its technical name: *invagination*.

Then, understand, finally, that if you'd been born with the ability
to operate yourself like a puppet, & pull yourself outside-in
by drawing your head down into your belly & out
through your foot, to invert your once-vibrant
body into an empty sock, how many times
you would have done exactly that.

Fight or Flight

if only the danger were the unseen

        cutting-away of daylight

crouched in the brush

                then   maybe

a silent closing-in

        a clouting   & an amber gaze

would hold me   dilated

      in my raptured knowing

              of a throat untethered

           from its million-year-unrest—

Anatomy of a Fustercluck

It's thanks to crime scenes like this
that I sometimes dread people,
particularly the way they flock to orange pylons,
fluster in clumps like maimed birds,
and hatch out stories,
which are always either parboiled in half-truths,
or scrambled by hypocrisy.

Take that camera-laden busy-body, for instance,
piqued there, barely disguising her hope
of spawning a murmuration—
donning her intrepidly purple polo,
she's the self-declared ruler
of the pecking order that's been bred into us
for the engendering of our chronicles:

Clearly, she knows how to swaddle her offspring
with ample pageantry
to ensure the stork's swift delivery
of her inchoate prince.

Like Cronus, her Titan predecessor,
who swallowed up his own children
to thwart the prophecy of his time-driven demise,
she's devouring a flood of raw peptides
from the sea-thick breeze
wafting right past the preoccupied deputy,
to sate her enduring appetite
for stone-cold lies.

Meanwhile, that blond-haired man
in the short shorts and flip-flops,
fixated on his faux-gold wristwatch,
has been pacing this whole time
on the cluster's fringe,
completely cracked.

If you ask me,
he's as guilty as the day is long.

Imprisoned

Now is not the time
for my fettered   titanium lines—

no time for me to claim
I know a thing or two about life
as if I were anyone's keeper…

A "suicidally depressed" convict doing life for murder
petitioned my psychotherapist friend to treat him:

& so it was that with all the detached generosity
a wife & mother of three could muster   she rendered
a diagnosis of anti-social personality disorder
even as his icy eyes ignited in her a germ of lust
that razed every trace of her in a sudden flush

Now is really not the time for idle moralizing
about prisoners   or locks & keys   as if
there were any kind of justice in poetry

It's not the time for tying up loose ends
saving pennies for rainy days   or chrysalizing
our wrinkly little walnut meats to pupate belief
in the virtue of counting the hours

Now   the dragon is awake
blinking in the daylight of withering dreams
wagging her head in a gnashing rage

Lupercalia

We probe into the distant   wintry
rest of white oaks & umbrella pines

moonlit with longing to thrill
in the feral   hesitant glints

that crack the black tourmaline cold
our eyes pursuing their penumbrae

until the brink of blindness   reaching
for our bloodline of lost

infidel selves   still bound
to the night's crystalline tenors

As our illicit   newborn brothers were
abandoned to the Tiber   & delivered

keening for milk   to their mongrel lives
we   too   were borne by a savage river

to a mother waiting on the Palatine shore

Matthew in the Fountain
August 1999, age 14 months

In the spray's scattering
of afternoon rays
      you pass before the sun
a toddling pointed-toe satellite
eclipsing all
but its faint red ghost

Summer haloes you in sun-white down
mottling the concrete's cool glisten
like a memory from the womb

Watching the world swim into focus
in your smart brown eyes
      your round cheeks
flushing with the kisses of angels
showering from the sky   I realize
in a shutter's split-second
            I've traversed eternity

My child   you burst open my heart like the sun
bursts infinitely open each fountain drop

In Response to My 13 Year-Old Daughter's Letter

Apologize? For regretting your birth?

That the white dove of sarcasm
has officially fledged from your belly
alit on the canopy   & uncaged its crystal trill
comes to me as no surprise

But neither of us could have foreseen the power
your brooding would conceive of pencil & ire
before the moment you spat out   crumpled   & hand delivered
my saltwater baptism

Your own tears   now dried for hours   blaze for me
from the gold heart in your gray-green eyes
willing my belief that you truly didn't realize
I've been there your whole life

At sundown   I'm the one always stumbling through the wood
like some sort of village idiot   brandishing my dim lantern
at the giant pines   as if I might catch them in the act
of uprooting themselves   & slinking away

Though you flit by & vanish into the trees
in a flash I can barely make out as a memory
your trace among the cedars & silvertips remains as innate in me
as the wolf's way to her newborn cub's whimper

Two months early
yet already ripe for the triumph
& pain only the fiercest have dared to carry in one body
you were born to fly from me—

& so   how could I ever be sorry
to know of finding you over & over again?

How to Take an Amazing Photo of a Solar Eclipse

First,
get knocked up,
plan a wedding in three months
and waddle down the aisle in white pumps
that fit you when you bought them.

Gain a total of forty-eight pounds
while throwing up for forty weeks,
and give birth to a nine-pound baby boy,
who is bigger and cries louder than any other
newborn in the maternity ward.

After you blink once or twice,
find yourself moving across the country
for your husband's engineering job,
with three cats, the six-week old baby,
and all of their respective paraphernalia
crammed into a purple minivan.

Critical Step: *Raising Your Boy*
To do this, start learning more about more things than you knew existed;
begin appreciating that this cherubic, gorgeous,
but almost alien issue of your loins
sees individual ice crystals in distant clouds,
hears crickets chirping at dusk
over the sound of rush-hour traffic,
plays the piano with no lessons better than you ever will.

Have conversations with your boy (that he begins)
about the waxing gibbous moon
when he is still in diapers.

Don't freak out when he runs to the garage to feel the water main
every time someone flushes the toilet
for an entire year.

Realize that this otherworldly child means no slight
when the Valentine's Day card he makes for you in first grade says,
"Dear Mom, I love the plants from Chris Tuffli's science project."

Scoop your bottom jaw off the floor
when he inquires about how nerve impulses
not only respond to, but initiate thoughts
(you will have had about seven years
to prepare for this moment,
but your heart will still flutter dangerously).

Believe that you are the only one who notices
that he has decided not to "turn left"
during the ages of eight and nine.

Get comfortable slinging around terms
like *high-functioning autism, echolalia,
sensory integration dysfunction, perfect pitch*
and *freaking genius.*

Find a place deep in your understanding that "gets"
how he is not unloving, ungrateful, or deliberately obtuse,
but admirably, unprecedentedly honest and real.
Become very angry when his teachers and coaches
try to justify being put-out
and dare to assign blame to a child,
rather than consider how they, being the adults,
might assume responsibility
for their interactions with him.

Fall fiercely in love with your magnificent boy,
so that your heart screams, your scalp hurts,
and your vision blurs
in this unsympathetic, simple-minded world's injustice.
It will then be easy for you
to put aside your concerns about ruffling feathers,
making waves, and rocking boats.
You will do anything necessary
to arm your son to thrive, shine,
and find his own joy.

Trust in his gift of seeing every moment
in terms of geological time—
of constantly holding the cycles of mountains
rising up and eroding away in his mind's eye—
and strain in your every breath, step, and toss in your sleep
to grasp
how his world is wholly un-glossed over
by super-imposed paradigms.

Never try to propagandize him
into a semblance of societal expectation.

Never believe for an instant that you
should temper your awe of him.

When he is a teenager,
endure an epic tongue-lashing
from your superego,
then fork out the dough,
anyway,
for the camera of his dreams.

An Elegy for Birds & Bees

> "When a woman pretends to press her life down into a nice, tidy little package, all she accomplishes is spring-loading all her vital energy down into shadow. 'Fine. I'm fine,' such a woman says... Then one day, we hear she has taken up with a piccolo player and has run off to Tippicanoe (sic) to be a pool hall queen..."
> Clarissa Pinkola Estés

over & over in habitual drone
i repeat a phrase in my mind that no one knows i say
because i have not told
i am saying *i'm done*
but this *being done*
is how i know i will never *be done*
though my climbing son
a speck eighty feet high in a skyline of swaying cedars
can heft the storm clouds away
from his own silvery horizon
& my seeking daughter
has tenacity enough   without me
to prize out four leaf clovers
from speciously green reaches
        but i will never release
this breath of finality that i keep
choked in my throat behind earnest songs for my children
no   & i will swallow the rising bile
when the Northern Flicker perches
on our aluminum chimney top   puffed-up
so proud in those marrow-less bones
of his impervious skull's clever   territorial ricocheting

being done happened
within my own sinew-lined pelvis
the cracked bowl
filled   drained   & refilled
with meticulously rich essences

long after anything living had been fed
the relentlessly heavy   gnawing
red slough of losing myself
to nothing   for nothing
frightened me
       & so   i had the offending flesh cut out
the fossilized rind that was left is now locked
with its un-told stories
beneath eons of hardened sediments

this *being done* happens in spring
while i am driving alone
it happens quickly
in instants of lapsed attention
in overzealous moments of stony apathy
when windshield wipers stick unexpectedly
or when sudden   pink shafts of evening sun
transmute newborn lambs bucking
for tender grass & mother's milk
into silhouettes haunting the roadside
      the *being done*
is all these countless   fleeting deaths
i tear into strips   soak in chewed glue
& fashion together to house myself
in a prodigal   crinkled   purgatorial prune

these tiny   stinging   imprudent suicides
should all be spirited away from their haughty blooms
& borne into the ancient hive
clutched industriously
to the undersides of fuzzy exoskeletons
      there   my secret   greedy orchestrations
would become coded in sacred routines
my life programmed in dance
& propagated by ecstatic waggles & fastidious figure eights

to a crescendo of communal comprehension
of the one   seminal purpose
of the *being done* that shall be

done at all costs
the Queen's Royal Jelly must be
sealed with wax in her hexagonal vaults

Instead

'if i decided to stop being a poet
what would i do instead?'   i asked
(my husband) the other night

the other night when it was late
it was too late to start cooking dinner
& the cattle dog   who lives for order

requires order   & feels its lack
like her hackles feel static   she was pacing
between us   resorting to vocal admonishments

to higher-than-usual-pitched chortling   cajoling
someone to get with the program   the other night
after gymnastics   & martial arts   & driving

driving in gridlock on multiple highways
after the shopping wasn't done
after—& we were too hungry to cook dinner—

after hunger became the side dish of the night
after my husband had worked all day
& beer number three hadn't staved off his hunger

& hunger was a side dish   the kids snacked
on chips   & played redundant games on their phones
& the floor was unswept   the dog was anxious

her nails clicked on the unkempt floor
the cat meowed to be fed   the shopping wasn't done
& so a can of tuna was cracked

the cat's bowl was filled   & we gave the dog the juice
the dog lapped   then she went back to clicking
& minutes ticked another hour

while my fingers ticking on the keyboard
whooped up a frenzy of words on the screen
with hurricane intensity they swirled

they dispelled into wisps against cold fronts
& re-galvanized in isolated updrafts   but rained nothing
because meaning always slips drily away from the words

& escapes like sly prey into the woods   because the words
bravely give chase   but they were never cut out for this hunt
& they get lost   & hungry

they go hungry like an injured wolf separated from its pack
like a cattle dog lacking order   & teenagers not-talking on phones
like groceries that can't shop for themselves

like the cat settling for tuna
well   not like that
like clacking keyboards churning up dry storms

like computer screens adrift
at the mercy of tidal waves of hunters
& peckers   & especially *delete*-ers

    like a poet who can't do anything instead

like the *shift* key   & the *alt* key
like the fourth beer needs to be the *ctrl* + *alt* + *delete* keys
like *delete* is a kind of key

they go hungry

like a husband

Brave

Some things leave no room for misunderstanding,
like your climbs to the tops of towering pines,
and your belief that you can never cry.

At age five, you dream of a woman
with wings like a bat dressed all in black.
She swoops down, grabs you, pins you in her lap,
and while hitting you over and over, she's whispering
that it will end when you stop struggling;
so you pretend to relax until her grip loosens
and then you fight to escape, but each time
her strength overwhelms you. It takes
several beatings before you realize
she is trying to help you, she is teaching you
how to be brave—
how to be so still
that you can let yourself have no feeling
when the scratchy hands are pressing into you,
like the night lets itself be swallowed by darkness.

An eight-year-old now, you're standing
outside their locked bedroom door, waiting
for your mother to call to you
as he yells his nonsense, rips out drawers,
and slams the walls with his fists.
When something made of glass shatters
against the vanity, her cry of surprise
convinces you to call the police.
They come and go in a flash—
barely pausing to ruffle your hair
and chuckle
that it was all "just a misunderstanding"—
and they leave you there,
to keep being unseen.

For most of the schoolyear,
at age eleven, you are chronically ill:
the oozing, itching, gray-swollen chickenpox lesions
that make you potently untouchable,
lead to an infiltration of fevers, flooded lungs,
and inflamed tonsils and ears
that hold you prisoner from the inside,
but soon you come to know your captors
as the oddly loyal, untiring allies
who keep you warded at night, for months.
Your classmates are jealous, though,
that you still make passing grades
in your constant absence from school—
on the phone, they accuse you of faking,
and you can't help the feeling, either,
that being sick really is a kind of cheating,
like getting something you want
without doing anything to earn it.

Mom is taking you to open a bank account
with your own passbook, though you're just twelve
(her eyes are still swollen from crying yesterday),
so you can sign for the money you'll need to get
yourself and your little brother to the airport
to fly to an uncle you barely know in New York,
if she either goes missing, or you find her dead,
because, as she's confided to you—
and you have no reason not to believe it—
your father vowed to kill her.
For the next three years, then (she doesn't know),
you skip lunch at school and save the money
to deposit into the "plane ticket" account.
No, she never gets murdered,
maybe even because you always keep watch,

like the kind of parent you'd want to be would,
even after your father finally moves out
during the same summer you get your tonsils
(and the disease they harbored) removed.

You're now proving to be a picture of health
(though you bear the hunger of indignity, standing
in lines in the school gym for government hand-outs
of peanut butter, processed cheese and expired bread),
because you can run like no one else.
You are your soccer coach's favorite, you believe,
because you are tough, and you work the hardest.
He makes a fuss over you like you are special,
takes you out for ice cream, has you come along
on fishing trips with his sons, and invites
you over for dinner, or to stay the night,
and you never consider he'll expect you to repay him
for these casual, kind gestures, until
he's suddenly always touching and hugging you
as if it is his right, and even though you make sure
only to be in public places with him,
in plain sight of your teammates' parents,
you can't discourage his lewd hovering,
or his propositions (which he thinks are charming)
for you to fuck him in the back of his van.
Somebody should be watching!
Somebody should be watching!
People are watching, but they only see
the things that have no need
for invisibility, like the crude posturing
of a man just being a man—

just someone who reserves
the Scouts' clubhouse through Parks and Rec

for a "team meeting" that you feel obligated to attend;
someone who waits on a weekday evening
in a prefab aluminum building
with the lights dimmed
for a fifteen-year-old girl to enter alone,
while, at home, his own kids watch T.V.,
and his wife keeps his dinner warm.

Some things leave no room for misunderstanding—

like the lust throbbing in a man's neck,
the presumption gleaming in his eyes,
and the fact that wrongs always pile upon wrongs
in the same way he now heaps this assault from behind,
with his thick hands fumbling for your breasts,
on top of his preposterous lie;

and so when he leans in with his belly
and his cock stiffens against the small of your back,
a scream gets trapped in your throat,
and you find yourself struggling wildly—
you elbow him hard in the ribs,
then rear up and ram your head into his chin,
and somehow stun him long enough
to get away—

you get away,
but leaving yourself there
unseen in the dark
doesn't ever feel brave.

Prologue to My Birth

This is neither a beginning
nor the prophecy of an ending
for beginnings & endings are lies
told to the once-living

it is not the exemplifying
of the aberrations the alchemists made
when they dethroned our Divine Queen
& transmuted her golden honey
into their iron pyrite philosophy
that left us to wither
inside our stunned husks

& so   this is the emptying
of our errant devotion
to the denial of bodily hunger

the sanctified unbelieving
in fairytales of heavenly salvation

& it is the vital refilling
of infants' gaping mouths
with earthly fortitude

& here   now   is the weeping

for our birth-story   interred
with our long-dead mothers
who delivered us
& secured our velvety   aboriginal flesh
to their warm breasts—

the saline unleashing
to purify our *Logos*
our will to creation   our innate need
to manifest our god-selves

it is the recovering
of the Life that was severed from our psyches
when it was reduced to a Word
& uttered   bereft of melody—

the unrepressed singing
Artemis awake from her slumber
beneath her ruined Temple in Ephesus

at last   this is the extricating
of shame that made our tongues
untie us from our Mother's holy earth
& swayed our ears to scorn her winged songs
even as she kept flying back to us
ever thick-limbed & fragrant
with nourishment from lavender blooms
solely that we should swell in our birthing cells
gorged on her royal jelly

This poem is my body
embryonic   translucent
distended with new hope

it is my luminous   black eyes
grown huge with their memory
of who I am

Rhapsody in Bone

Beneath the frozen fathoms of the sea,
a maiden's body swells in rhapsody;
her father made her sustenance for fish
and creatures yet unseen by human eyes,
who feed until the carrion is spent.

The maiden's bones roll over with the tide,
entwined with deep-sea coral colonies,
and where her eyes were, now are dwellings kept
by denizens who have no need of light
beneath the frozen fathoms of the sea.

Though water's currents quell the dolphins' calls,
the doleful cries her fecund corpse intones
uncoil the sodden hearts of others' souls,
while hers, forsaken, flounders in the dark.
A maiden's body belts a rhapsody,

because her father threw her from a cliff:
Butt-hurt that she'd flat-out refused to stroke
his ego (teeny-peeny sack, he was,
of whims that changed as often as the winds),
her father made her sustenance for fish,

yet could not stop his daughter's sunken bones
from breathing sirens' cantos on the waves
and luring hunters to her icy grave—
that home to lonely spirits of the depths,
and creatures yet unseen by human eyes!

A hunter plunks his line into the sea,
where deep below, a bony treasury
still bears the stench of murder's milky dregs,
a tangy lunch for urchins clinging fast,
who feed until the carrion is spent.

Upon the swaying surf the hunter waits
with hero's grit, 'til suddenly, a lurch—
he's hooked the skeleton woman's rib! *This catch
has heft suggesting banquets fit for kings,
who feed until the carrion is spent!*

Oy veh! He hoists her bones onto his skiff
and shits his britches fearing he's been cursed
by Death, herself, arisen from the depths—
her salt-worn bones a host for writhing eels,
and creatures yet unseen by human eyes!

Try as he may to toss her back, he finds
her long front teeth affixed—and can't deny
this woman he's revived deserves to live:
those naked, tangled limbs, her smooth, bald head...
Her father made her sustenance for fish,

yet could not stop his daughter's sunken bones
from going viral with their exposés—
though water tries to quash the dolphins' calls—
for songs of fuckhead fathers make us sick,
when maidens' bodies swell in rhapsody!

Though many hunters know the songs of bones,
scarce few boast true cajones, fewer still
behold the face of Death with steadfast gaze,
and grow to love and keep all she became
beneath the frozen fathoms of the sea.

Epitaph
    For JPM

    "We have been taught that death is always followed by more death. It is simply not so, death is always in the process of incubating new life, even when one's existence has been cut down to the bones."
                  Clarissa Pinkola Estés

    Drawn down in my dream
    beneath this artifice of death   I was
    looking in the shadows for you
    but I lost my way

In this frozen ruin leveled by your suicide
the scarce words you'd sealed with waxy scorn
wrought a silence
known only to the forsaken

    The passageways were laden
    with diorite & lapis lazuli figurines
    of Anubis & Horus   the ubiquitous jackal
    ushering my vague corpse
    past his brother's omniscient   weeping eyes

    Shards everywhere rent from the heavens
    were waiting   disembodied   to be renamed
    but the Curator's censure
    of their reckless   fledgling deaths
    was cast in twilit bronze

I fully believed that you had spurned your river journey
thumbed your nose at Osiris' fertile valley
& sunken

    In my loneliness
    I leaned against a granite sunk relief
    of some forgotten pharaoh
    & fitfully dozed

Steeped to my skeletal roots in the fallen
chaos of loss   my tear-starved blood
dried to dust on the sky's halted breath
I slept
until daylight returned
to unearth me

    My vault opened   & you filtered in
        your warmth on my cheek

I awoke   my sarcophagus glittering
& I knew
you were my sun

    §

A headstone bears your name

but marks a stranger   broken
beyond my art to fathom
much less to condemn

so I will try to be a heart of light
that steals on your veil of whispers

rising from the arcane night

Alabaster

I am a pink rose petal's pale glow

black ash tamped in furrows
between the breaths of the living
& the droning of the dead

the dawn's blush unfurling over sand dunes

& seagulls soaring on thermal spirits
of iodine   salt   & shellfish

& sometimes   scattering in the wind
I can't find where everything else ends   & I begin

Now rising from the morning hush   this cloud of me
speaks to the red tail hawk perched on a streetlamp
& tells her I'm fine   because I'm still not sure
how to talk about not being fine

I am an instar   trying to be
the clearest version of myself   to sculpt
a final skin of lucent crystal

so that when you come to see my cinder eyes
glinting diamond dust   I will be
the embered dusk bleeding into the sea

& you will know the truth of me

Tempted

Were our names droned above deck   nobody
would cock a head toward the source   tempted
into a double take   Leaden   ignored
a slithering of esses would bumble
in the ship's rigging above those joyless
seadogs numbed by the sail-blunted breeze   Sing!

Fly tempestuous from your caves   & sing
of maiden savagery   such that nobody
would foil the sail's dulcet urgings!   Joyless
& tiresome are the notes we've been tempted
to low like abject ghosts whose every fumble
on the floorboards is one more creak ignored

Though we were hushed by the winds & ignored
by the foam drifts   I long again to sing
for Sirenum   to see fresh souls stumble
upon our craggy strand that nobody
calls the way home   Oh   how I stir   tempted
to perform my numbers on their joyless

furrowed brows   anesthetized by joyless
vermin-corked rum—fruitless   fusty   ignored!
The more pallid they are   the more tempted
I am by my primal discords to sing!
Since these lone slogs have yet wiled nobody
into pursuing my briny mumble

it seems all the same   then   I should grumble
presumptions to spur you   too   my joyless
sisters   to shed your stone tails   Nobody
used to cast us off   sand-crusted   ignored
milked dry of our mantic cores!   When I sing
of our sweet shame   you'll be sorely tempted

to hear—chances are good you'll be tempted
to strap on feet   if need be   to rumble
shipboard dins to hound those fellows   & sing
them to proper attention!   Our joyless
slumber will not stay shrouded & ignored
when we wake up from being nobody!

Tempted   joyless Salts   are ye   to strike for
yon fair shore?   Heed lest ye crumble   ignored!
Nobody will sing while my sisters sleep...

Live Feed from the SW Florida Eagle Cam
For E9, Born December 31, 2016

1.
Everything
must first have been

a nameless billowing
in the silent house

of *before*   until its voice
yolk-forged   could wrest

a pyroclastic mouth
sufficient to speak birth's

dialect of brokenness

2.
I watched the possibility of you
cradled sixty feet high in a Slash Pine

become a five-day-old
white fluff-bundle of spunk

& open-beaked ferocity   You
command the ripping impulse

that strips off the fish's silver skin
midriff to tail   with one   swift

grip & flexion   exposing
the host's fleshy glisten

of lipid-pink life to be flaked
& held to your tiny maw's tip

3.
Before this feeding   I think
nothing had yet been born

whose name was *Tenderness*—

       no one to bring this warmth
of tastes & swallows growing ever

heavier in your belly & on your lids
to bear you to your imperative sleep:

Dream   *Little One*   in the haven
of your father's stalwart breast!

Dream of wings outstretched
on the azure's salt-breath!

Stephanie L. Harper lives with her husband, two teen children, and a dwindling geriatric menagerie in Hillsboro, OR., where she performs the beatified deeds of a home schooling parent and writes poetry, sometimes simultaneously. She graduated from Grinnell College with a B.A. in English and German, and from the University of Wisconsin-Madison with an M.A. in German literature; and excelled in the thorough disillusionment module of her Master of Divinity program at the Northwest House of Theological Studies (in consortium with the Pacific School of Religion in Berkley, CA). Stephanie is a Pushcart Prize nominee, and her poems appear in *Stories That Need to Be Told* (a TulipTree Publishing, LLC anthology), *Slippery Elm Literary Journal, Rattle magazine's Ekphrastic Challenge, Figroot, Califragile, Harbinger Asylum, Panoply, The Ibis Head Review,* and elsewhere.

www.ingramcontent.com/pod-product-compliance
Lightning Source LLC
LaVergne TN
LVHW041509070426
835507LV00012B/1451